PRESIDENTIAL PETS

The Weird, Wacky, Little, Big, Scary, Strange Animals That Have Lived in the White House

By Julia Moberg

Illustrated by Jeff Albrecht Studios

imagine!
Publishing

For my brother, Michael—J.M.

An Imagine Book
Published by Charlesbridge
9 Galen Street, Watertown, MA 02472
(617) 926-0329
www.charlesbridge.com

First paperback edition 2016
Text copyright © 2012 by Julia Moberg.
Illustrations copyright © 2012 by Charlesbridge Publishing, Inc.
Cover and interior design by Melissa Gerber.
Printed in China, March 2016.

The publisher does not have any control over and does not assume any responsibility for author or third-party websites or their content.

Library of Congress Cataloging-in-Publication Data
Moberg, Julia.
 Presidential pets / by Julia Moberg ; illustrated by Jeff Albrecht.
    p. cm. — (An imagine book)
 Includes index.
 ISBN 978-1-936140-79-4 (reinforced for library use)
 ISBN 978-1-62354-086-9 (softcover)
 ISBN 978-1-60734-582-4 (ebook pdf)
1. Presidents' pets—United States—Juvenile literature. 2.
Presidents—United States—Biography—Juvenile literature. 3. Pets—United
States—Juvenile literature. I. Albrecht, Jeff, ill. II. Title.
 E176.48.M62 2012
 973—dc23   2011047785

hc 10 9 8 7 6 5 4
sc 10 9 8 7 6 5 4 3

Many of our presidents
Owned several pets
That history books
Sometimes forget.
Yes, they had dogs,
Cats, fish, and birds,
But several of them
Owned pets more absurd.
Bear cubs, for instance,
Lived at the White House.
One president even
Had a pet mouse!
Goats, cows, raccoons,
Horses galore,
Turkeys and snakes,
A parrot that swore!
So turn the page
If you want to hear more . . .

A friend from France
Sent George some hounds—
Dogs of good breed
That were sure to astound.
Unfortunately for George,
He asked his friend John
To escort the hounds
On the boat into town.
The dogs behaved badly
On the boat ride home,
So John left them all
At the harbor alone.

Tell Me More!

* A young John Quincy Adams (our sixth president) was the hounds' escort. We don't know if Washington ever forgave John for leaving them at the New York harbor. They were eventually found.
* Washington crossed the dogs with his black and tan hounds and created a new breed: the American foxhound.
* Washington was constantly creating new breeds of dogs, horses, and mules. He dreamed of creating a superior dog with exceptional speed, brains, and heightened senses.
* At his Mount Vernon plantation, Washington had horses, dogs, pigs, sheep, mules, turkeys, chickens, cows, and oxen.
* Martha Washington owned a parrot.
* There are many places named after Washington, including the nation's capital, the state, thirty-one counties, and at least seventeen communities.
* After his presidency, Washington realized that slavery was morally wrong. Before his death, he freed all of his slaves.

Presidential Stats

TERM: 1789–1797

FIRST LADY: Martha Dandridge Custis Washington

VICE PRESIDENT: John Adams

POLITICAL PARTY: Federalist

BORN: February 22, 1732 (Westmoreland County, Virginia)

DIED: December 14, 1799 (Mount Vernon, Virginia)

OCCUPATION BEFORE PRESIDENCY: Plantation farmer, general and commander-in-chief of the Continental Army, president of the Constitutional Convention

NICKNAME: The Father of His Country

Accomplishments & Events

* Supervised the formation of the National Bank.
* Passed the Bill of Rights (the first ten amendments to the Constitution).
* Admitted Vermont, Kentucky, and Tennessee into the Union.

JOHN ADAMS

Guess what the First Lady
Named one of her pets?
Not Fido or Spot
Or Biscuit or Jet.
No, the mixed-breed dog,
Much to everyone's chagrin,
Was unfortunately given
The odd name Satan.
John preferred horses;
He had his own mare
With a dark shiny hide
And flowing black hair.
Her name was Cleopatra.
John rode her 'round town,
And had stables built
On the White House grounds.

Presidential Stats

TERM: 1797–1801
FIRST LADY: Abigail Smith Adams
VICE PRESIDENT: Thomas Jefferson
POLITICAL PARTY: Federalist
BORN: October 30, 1735 (Braintree, Massachusetts)
DIED: July 4, 1826 (Braintree, Massachusetts)
OCCUPATION BEFORE PRESIDENCY: Lawyer, vice president of the United States
NICKNAME: The Colossus of Independence

Tell Me More!

✳ In addition to Satan, Abigail Adams also had a mixed-breed dog named Juno.

✳ Built in 1800, the first White House stable house was located on the corner of 14th and G Streets.

✳ Because Adams traveled often, he and Abigail would sometimes spend years apart. Between 1762 and 1801, they exchanged over 1,100 letters.

✳ Adams was the first president whose son (John Quincy Adams) also became president.

Accomplishments & Events

✳ Served on the committee that wrote the Declaration of Independence.

✳ Passed the Alien and Sedition Acts, four bills that placed restrictions on foreign citizens.

✳ Refused to bribe the French government with money in exchange for a peaceful agreement in a conflict known as the XYZ Affair, which almost resulted in a war between the two countries.

THOMAS JEFFERSON

Thomas Jefferson
Sent a team out West,
And two grizzly bear cubs
Were found on the quest.
He built them a cage
On the White House front lawn,
And sometimes he'd walk them
On leashes at dawn.
The two baby bears
Became quite a sensation.
They represented land
And the growth of our nation.

Presidential Stats

TERM: 1801–1809

FIRST LADY: Martha Wayles Skelton Jefferson (died before Thomas took office)

VICE PRESIDENT: Aaron Burr (first term), George Clinton (second term)

POLITICAL PARTY: Democrat-Republican

BORN: April 13, 1743 (Goochland County—now Albemarle County—Virginia)

DIED: July 4, 1826 (Monticello, Virginia)—Jefferson died approximately five hours before John Adams

OCCUPATION BEFORE PRESIDENCY: Lawyer, governor of Virginia, minister to France, secretary of state, vice president of the United States

NICKNAME: Man of the People

Tell Me More!

✳ The exploration team led by Lieutenant Zebulon Pike accidentally crossed into Spanish territory near the Arkansas River. The team was arrested by Spanish authorities. As Pike was being escorted back to U.S. territory, he purchased the bear cubs from a local inhabitant.

✳ When the bears grew too big for their White House cages, Jefferson sent them to live at a museum. (Yes, a museum! Not a zoo.)

✳ Jefferson also had a mockingbird named Dick who sometimes rode on his shoulder. When nobody was around, he would open Dick's cage and let him fly freely around his office. Jefferson also owned several dogs.

✳ Jefferson was the key author of the Declaration of Independence, written in 1776.

✳ After traveling through Europe as the minister to France, Jefferson introduced pasta and ice cream to the country.

Accomplishments & Events

✳ Made the Louisiana Purchase (827,987 square miles of land) and doubled the size of the United States.

✳ Authorized the Lewis and Clark expedition that explored the land bought in the Louisiana Purchase.

✳ Admitted Ohio into the Union.

James Madison

In 1812,
The British came
And sent the White House
Up in flames.
Afraid for her parrot,
The First Lady sent
Uncle Willy to live
With the French Consulate.
Meanwhile, the president
Was rallying troops.
He guarded the ports
And sent ships out in groups.
He defeated the Brits
And resumed government dealings
That eventually led
To the Era of Good Feelings.

Tell Me More!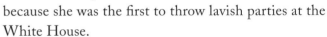

* The Era of Good Feelings was a period of peace that lasted approximately from 1816 to 1824. Although Madison was president at the beginning of this time period, his successor, James Monroe, is best known as the Era of Good Feelings President.

* Madison had a flock of sheep that grazed on the White House lawn.

* Madison is the smallest president to date. He was five feet, four inches tall and weighed only a hundred pounds!

* Dolley Madison is often called the *First* First Lady because she was the first to throw lavish parties at the White House.

Presidential Stats

TERM: 1809–1817

FIRST LADY: Dorothy (Dolley) Payne Todd Madison

VICE PRESIDENT: George Clinton (first term), Elbridge Gerry (second term)

POLITICAL PARTY: Democrat-Republican

BORN: March 16, 1751 (Port Conway, Virginia)

DIED: June 28, 1836 (Montpelier Estate, Virginia)

OCCUPATION BEFORE PRESIDENCY: Lawyer, member of the U.S. House of Representatives, secretary of state

NICKNAME: Father of the Constitution

Accomplishments & Events

* Was the youngest delegate at the Continental Congress and a key contributor to the United States Constitution and the Bill of Rights.

* Authored the Federalist Papers, eighty-five articles promoting the ratification of the Constitution. He wrote these with Alexander Hamilton and John Jay.

* Went to war with Great Britain, officially ending all economic dependence on the British.

* Admitted Louisiana and Indiana into the Union.

JAMES MONROE

Monroe had a spaniel,
Some historians claim,
But nobody knows
The poor puppy's name.
He was called Buddy,
Many sources detail,
But it isn't clear
If he was male or female.

Tell Me More!

✳ The Monroes may have also owned a sheepdog.

✳ After being damaged during the War of 1812, the White House was reopened during Monroe's presidency. Its sandstone exterior was painted white the year he became president.

✳ Monroe and his wife, Elizabeth, threw the first wedding at the White House for their seventeen-year-old daughter Maria.

✳ Monroe was the third president to die on the Fourth of July. John Adams and Thomas Jefferson also passed away on the nation's birthday.

Presidential Stats

TERM: 1817–1825

FIRST LADY: Elizabeth Jones Kortright Monroe

VICE PRESIDENT: Daniel D. Tompkins

POLITICAL PARTY: Democrat-Republican

BORN: April 28, 1758 (Westmoreland County, Virginia)

DIED: July 4, 1831 (New York, New York)

OCCUPATION BEFORE PRESIDENCY: Lawyer

NICKNAME: The Era of Good Feelings President

Accomplishments & Events

✳ Established the Monroe Doctrine, preventing foreign nations from settling in America.

✳ Passed the Missouri Compromise that admitted Missouri into the Union as a slave state and Maine as a free state. As a result, the Mason-Dixon Line was extended.

✳ Helped form the American Colonization Society, which sent freed slaves to the newly formed African country of Liberia.

✳ Admitted Mississippi, Illinois, Alabama, Maine, and Missouri into the Union.

JOHN QUINCY ADAMS

The very same Frenchman
Who sent Washington hounds
Gave John Quincy Adams
A pet for the grounds.
It arrived at the house
One fine summer day;
It wasn't a dog
Or a cat or blue jay.
When John opened the box
That arrived via freighter,
He was startled to find
A pet alligator.
Not sure where to keep it,
Not sure what to do,
He found it a home
In a White House bathroom!
When friends came to visit
John let them explore.
Imagine their fright
When they opened *that* door!

Tell Me More!

✳ The alligator lived in the East Room bathroom for two months before returning to France.

✳ First Lady Louisa Adams raised silkworms at the White House. She had gowns made from the silk they produced.

✳ In the mornings, Adams would go skinny-dipping in the Potomac River. One day his clothes were stolen and he had to ask a stranger to run to the White House to get him another suit!

✳ Adams read the Bible cover to cover every year.

Presidential Stats

TERM: 1825–1829

FIRST LADY: Louisa Catherine Johnson Adams

VICE PRESIDENT: John C. Calhoun

POLITICAL PARTY: Democrat-Republican

BORN: July 11, 1767 (Braintree—now Quincy—Massachusetts)

DIED: February 23, 1848 (Washington, DC)

OCCUPATION BEFORE PRESIDENCY: Lawyer, minister to Great Britain, the Netherlands, Russia, and Prussia, member of the U.S. Senate and the U.S. House of Representatives, secretary of state

NICKNAME: Old Man Eloquent

Accomplishments & Events

✳ Placed high taxes on imported items from foreign countries to protect domestic industries.

✳ Improved America's transportation system (roads and canals).

✳ The only president to serve in the House of Representatives *after* holding office. In the House, he argued the famous *Amistad* case before the Supreme Court and won, freeing thirty-five kidnapped Africans.

ANDREW JACKSON

Jackson's parrot, Poll,
Who whistled and spoke,
Had a bad habit
When she was provoked.
The president, it seems,
She often mimed,
And as a result
She cussed all the time!
Poll swore up a storm
In English and Spanish;
This often resulted
In her being banished.

Tell Me More!

* At Jackson's own funeral, Poll had to be removed because she wouldn't stop swearing.

* Jackson also owned several horses, including his favorite, Sam Patch. The horse was named after an American daredevil who was the first person to jump over Niagara Falls and survive.

* Jackson raised roosters.

* Jackson was the first president to ride on a railroad train.

Presidential Stats

TERM: 1829–1837

FIRST LADY: Rachel Donelson Robards Jackson (died before Jackson took office) and Emily Donelson (Jackson's niece who served as First Lady)

VICE PRESIDENT: John C. Calhoun (first term), Martin Van Buren (second term)

POLITICAL PARTY: Democrat-Republican (first term); Democrat (second term)

BORN: March 15, 1767 (Waxhaws area, North Carolina–South Carolina border)

DIED: June 4, 1845 (Nashville, Tennessee)

OCCUPATION BEFORE PRESIDENCY: Lawyer, soldier, member of the U.S. House of Representatives and the U.S. Senate

NICKNAME: Old Hickory

Accomplishments & Events

* Signed the Indian Removal Act of 1830 to move several American Indian tribes from their land within existing states to unsettled land in the west. The perilous journey the tribes took to their new land is now known as the Trail of Tears.

* Worked toward abolishing the National Bank, which he saw as a threat to American liberties.

* Admitted Arkansas and Michigan into the Union.

MARTIN VAN BUREN

The Sultan of Oman
Sent the president a gift:
Two baby tigers
That caused quite a rift.
Van Buren insisted,
"They were gifted to *me*!"
But Congress claimed,
"They were gifted to *we*!"
They argued until
They were blue in the face,
So the tigers left home
For some much-needed space.
They went to the zoo
For some rest and relaxing.
Politicians, it seems,
Could be really quite taxing!

Presidential Stats

TERM: 1837–1841

FIRST LADY: Hannah Hoes Van Buren

VICE PRESIDENT: Richard M. Johnson

POLITICAL PARTY: Democrat

BORN: December 5, 1782 (Kinderhook, New York)

DIED: July 24, 1862 (Kinderhook, New York)

OCCUPATION BEFORE PRESIDENCY: Lawyer, member of the New York State Senate and U.S. Senate, governor of New York, secretary of state, vice president of the United States

NICKNAME: OK

Tell Me More!

✴ In addition to the tiger cubs, the Sultan of Oman sent Van Buren many other gifts. He was not allowed to accept gifts from any foreign leader, so they were handed over to Congress for safekeeping.

✴ Riding horses was Van Buren's favorite sport.

✴ Van Buren was the first president born in America. All presidents before him are considered to be British because they were born before the Declaration of Independence was signed.

✴ Van Buren spoke fluent Dutch.

Accomplishments & Events

✴ During his presidency, nine hundred banks collapsed, resulting in the Panic of 1837. In response, Van Buren established a federal treasury to protect government funds.

✴ Prevented Texas from being admitted into the Union because he did not want to expand slave territory or risk going to war with Mexico.

✴ Continued Andrew Jackson's removal of American Indians from their land.

WILLIAM HENRY HARRISON

William's goat Whiskers
Enjoyed life in DC.
He'd frolic about
Wherever he pleased.
And Sukey, his cow,
Was happy as punch
To lay in the sun
And munch on her lunch.
These two lived quite well
On the lawn where they grazed.
Too bad Bill was the prez
Only thirty-one days!

Tell Me More!

✳ Harrison's goat's full name was His Whiskers.

✳ Harrison gave the longest inaugural speech in U.S. history. On a cold rainy day in Washington, he spoke for almost two hours. Less than a month later, he died from pneumonia. He was the first president to die in office.

✳ Harrison is also the only president to study medicine.

✳ Harrison's father, Benjamin Harrison, a delegate from Virginia, was one of the Founding Fathers of the United States.

Presidential Stats

TERM: 1841

FIRST LADY: Anna Tuthill Symmes Harrison

VICE PRESIDENT: John Tyler

POLITICAL PARTY: Whig

BORN: February 9, 1773 (Berkeley Plantation, Charles City County, Virginia)

DIED: April 4, 1841 (Washington, DC)

OCCUPATION BEFORE PRESIDENCY: Soldier, member of the U.S. House of Representatives, Ohio State Senate, and U.S. Senate, minister to Columbia

NICKNAME: Old Tippecanoe

Accomplishments & Events

✳ As a soldier, was most known for his victory over a Shawnee chief at the Battle of Tippecanoe. He gained control of Indian territory, which allowed for colonization in the Northwest.

✳ Accomplished little as a president, since he was only in office for a month.

John Tyler

John Tyler's presidency
Was often quite harried;
His party refused him,
His popularity varied.
But First Lady Julia
Dressed to impress.
Whatever she wanted,
The president said yes.
He bought her a greyhound,
From Italy it came.
She'd take it for walks;
Le Beau was its name.
She also enjoyed
Riding 'round town
In a regal coach
(And expensive gowns)
Pulled by six horses
Of Arabian breed.
The newspapers claimed
She was spoiled indeed!

Tell Me More!

* Tyler's favorite horse was named the General. When his horse died, Tyler had a headstone placed on the grave that said "Here lies the body of my good horse 'The General.' For twenty years he bore me around the circuit of my practice, and in all that time he never made a blunder. Would that his master could say the same!"

* Tyler was the first president to marry while in office. He married Julia Gardiner two years after his first wife, Letitia Christian Tyler, passed away.

* Tyler's party (the Whigs) rejected him. His cabinet members changed so many times, he essentially became a president without a party.

Presidential Stats

TERM: 1841–1845

FIRST LADY: Letitia Christian Tyler and Julia Gardiner Tyler

VICE PRESIDENT: None

POLITICAL PARTY: Whig

BORN: March 29, 1790 (Greenway Plantation, Charles City County, Virginia)

DIED: January 18, 1862 (Richmond, Virginia)

OCCUPATION BEFORE PRESIDENCY: Lawyer, member of the U.S. House of Representatives and the U.S. Senate, governor of Virginia, vice president of the United States

NICKNAME: His Accidency

Accomplishments & Events

* Passed the Preemption Act of 1841 that allowed squatters to live on public lands.

* Signed the Webster-Ashburton Treaty that established the border between Maine and Canada.

* Admitted Florida into the Union.

JAMES KNOX POLK

On the family horse
Before he could walk,
James learned how to ride
Before he could talk.
Ironically, during
His presidential run
He was called the dark horse,
And his victory stunned.
Nobody thought that
He would win against Clay,
But he did, much to
The Whig Party's dismay.
Polk brought many horses
With him to DC,
But he didn't ride much.
He was way too busy!

Presidential Stats

TERM: 1845–1849

FIRST LADY: Sarah Childress Polk

VICE PRESIDENT: George M. Dallas

POLITICAL PARTY: Democrat

BORN: November 2, 1795 (Mecklenburg County, North Carolina)

DIED: June 15, 1849 (Nashville, Tennessee)

OCCUPATION BEFORE PRESIDENCY: Lawyer, member of the U.S. House of Representatives, Speaker of the House, governor of Tennessee

NICKNAME: Young Hickory

Tell Me More!

* Polk loved riding his horses, but his presidential duties took up too much time to allow him to ride very often.

* Polk was known as the dark horse during his candidacy because he seemed to be an unlikely presidential candidate. He defeated the Whig Party's front-runner, Henry Clay.

* Polk hosted the first Thanksgiving dinner at the White House.

* Polk oversaw the openings of the Smithsonian Institute and the U.S. Naval Academy.

Accomplishments & Events

* Signed a treaty with Great Britain that set the forty-ninth parallel (a circle of latitude) as the border between the United States and Canada. As a result, the United States gained land that later became Oregon, Montana, Washington, and Idaho.

* Went to war with Mexico in 1846, which resulted in the United States getting 500,000 square miles of land. This also set the Rio Grande River as the border between the two countries.

* Admitted Texas, Iowa, and Wisconsin into the Union.

ZACHARY TAYLOR

When Taylor became president,
His horse Whitey came along
And spent his days grazing
On the White House front lawn.
When friends came to call,
Poor Whitey did find
They'd snag a souvenir
From his horse-haired behind.
One strand or two
They'd take from his rear,
Till his once-full tail
Did disappear!

Tell Me More!

✳ Old Whitey was Taylor's favorite horse. They rode together during the Mexican-American War (1846–1848).

✳ Taylor also had a canary named Johnny Ty.

✳ After only sixteen months in office, Taylor became sick after eating milk and cherries at a Fourth of July celebration. He died suddenly a few days later. Old Whitey attended the funeral.

✳ James Madison was Taylor's second cousin.

Presidential Stats

TERM: 1849–1850

FIRST LADY: Margaret Mackall Smith Taylor

VICE PRESIDENT: Millard Fillmore

POLITICAL PARTY: Whig

BORN: November 24, 1784 (Montebello, Virginia)

DIED: July 9, 1850 (Washington, DC)

OCCUPATION BEFORE PRESIDENCY: Soldier

NICKNAME: Old Rough and Ready

Accomplishments & Events

✳ The nation's most famous Mexican-American War hero.

✳ Signed the Clayton-Bulwer Treaty with Great Britain that gave both countries equal control over canals built in Central America. It also prevented either country from colonizing Central America.

✳ Proposed to admit California and New Mexico into the Union as free states.

MILLARD FILLMORE

Millard Fillmore
Married his teacher,
But didn't own
Any furry-haired creatures.

Presidential Stats

TERM: 1850–1853

FIRST LADY: Abigail Powers Fillmore

VICE PRESIDENT: None

POLITICAL PARTY: Whig

BORN: January 7, 1800 (Locke Township—now Summerhill—New York)

DIED: March 8, 1874 (Buffalo, New York)

OCCUPATION BEFORE PRESIDENCY: Lawyer, member of the U.S. House of Representatives, vice president of the United States

NICKNAME: The American Louis-Philippe

Tell Me More!

✷ Even though Fillmore didn't have pets, he founded the Buffalo, NY, chapter of the American Society for the Prevention of Cruelty to Animals.

✷ While attending the New Hope Academy, Fillmore fell in love with his schoolteacher Abigail Powers, who was one year older than he was. They married several years later.

✷ Fillmore was born in a log cabin to a poor family.

✷ As a young boy, he was an indentured servant to a cloth maker. He purchased his freedom for $30.

Accomplishments & Events

✷ Purchased 30,000 square miles of land from Mexico, known as the Gadsden Purchase. The land is now part of Arizona and New Mexico.

✷ Signed the Kansas-Nebraska Act that overturned the Missouri Compromise, leaving the issue of slavery up to the settlers in those areas. This led to violent fights within the Kansas territory (known as "Bleeding Kansas").

✷ Was the first elected president not to be renominated by his party.

FRANKLIN PIERCE

Franklin got a gift
From Commodore Perry:
Two tiny sleeve pups,
Who were very hairy.
Of Japanese origin,
They were feisty as rockets,
And President Pierce
Carried one in his pocket.

Presidential Stats

TERM: 1853–1857

FIRST LADY: Jane Means Appleton Pierce

VICE PRESIDENT: William R. King (died before taking office)

POLITICAL PARTY: Democrat

BORN: November 23, 1804 (Hillsborough, New Hampshire)

DIED: October 8, 1869 (Concord, New Hampshire)

OCCUPATION BEFORE PRESIDENCY: Lawyer, member of the U.S. Senate and U.S. House of Representatives

NICKNAME: Handsome Frank

Tell Me More!

✳ It is not known for certain whether the puppies were given to Pierce or not. Rumor has it that he kept one of them for himself and gave the other to his friend Jefferson Davis. Davis later became the president of the Confederacy during the Civil War.

✳ Matthew C. Perry, who allegedly gave Pierce the puppies, was the commodore of the U.S. Navy. A commodore is an old naval ranking that doesn't exist anymore. (Today the equivalent ranking in the U.S. Navy is a senior captain.)

✳ Pierce was the first president to have a Christmas tree in the White House.

✳ Pierce delivered his inaugural address (3,329 words) from memory, without any notes.

Accomplishments & Events

✳ Did not like making presidential decisions, so he often let others make them instead.

✳ Enforced the Fugitive Slave Act that helped return fugitive slaves to their owners.

✳ Admitted California into the Union.

JAMES BUCHANAN

The King of Siam
Sent a package to James:
A gold sword, some tusks,
An ornate picture frame.
He included a letter
Asking permission to send
Two Thai elephants
To his American friend.
Now James enjoyed pets;
He was an animal guy.
He had a dog, Lara,
And two birds that could fly.
But the package came late,
After James left his rank,
So Lincoln wrote back,
"Thanks, but no thanks."

Tell Me More!

✵ Abraham Lincoln politely declined the elephants because he didn't feel the American climate was good for them.

✵ Buchanan's birds were bald eagles, and his dog was a Newfoundland.

✵ Buchanan was the only president who never married. While he was in office, his niece Harriet Lane served as his First Lady.

✵ Buchanan liked to throw sauerkraut and mashed potato parties.

Presidential Stats

TERM: 1857–1861

FIRST LADY: Harriet Rebecca Lane Johnston

VICE PRESIDENT: John C. Breckinridge

POLITICAL PARTY: Democrat

BORN: April 23, 1791 (Cove Gap, Pennsylvania)

DIED: June 1, 1868 (Lancaster, Pennsylvania)

OCCUPATION BEFORE PRESIDENCY: Lawyer, member of the U.S. House of Representatives and U.S. Senate, minister to Russia and Great Britain, secretary of state

NICKNAME: Old Buck

Accomplishments & Events

✵ Wanted to end the controversy surrounding slavery, and decided that the ruling would be made by the Supreme Court. In 1857, the Court decided that African-Americans and their descendants had no rights of citizenship in all territories.

✵ Denied states the right to secede from the country, but the secessionist leaders did not want to compromise. Alabama, Florida, Georgia, Louisiana, Mississippi, South Carolina, and Texas seceded from the Union against his jurisdiction.

✵ Admitted Minnesota, Oregon, and Kansas into the Union.

ABRAHAM LINCOLN

In the fall
Of 1863
A turkey was given
For a First Family feast.
The bird became friends
With ten-year-old Tad,
Who barged in on a meeting
To talk to his dad.
Tad begged and he pleaded
For Jack's life to be spared.
"Okay, we won't eat him!"
Lincoln declared.
Right on the spot,
He wrote a reprieve
Sparing Jack's life.
Tad was relieved!
Jack lived out his days,
Happy to roam
The White House grounds,
His permanent home.

Tell Me More!

✴ While there are no historical records of Lincoln sparing the turkey's life, the story has been turned into a modern tradition. Every year since 1989, a turkey given to the president is pardoned in a ceremony at the White House.

✴ When the Lincolns moved to the White House, they had to leave their dog, Fido, behind. Fido was scared of loud noises, especially trains. The family feared that Fido would not survive the train trip to Washington, DC.

✴ The Lincolns got a little dog named Jip after they moved. Jip sometimes ate lunch with the president. He would sit on Lincoln's lap and was fed treats.

✴ Lincoln's son Tad (his real name was Thomas) owned two goats, Nanny and Nanko. They lived at the White House and were always chewing the furniture and eating the flowerbeds.

✴ Lincoln had a pet pig, and the family also had ponies, rabbits, and cats.

✴ On April 14, 1865, Lincoln was shot by John Wilkes Booth at Ford's Theater in Washington, DC. He was taken to Peterson's Boarding House across the street where he later died.

Accomplishments & Events

✴ On April 12, 1861, the Civil War started. In response, Lincoln had over 18,000 rebel leaders arrested and held in prisons.

✴ On January 1, 1863, issued the Emancipation Proclamation declaring slavery unlawful in Confederate states.

✴ On November 19, 1863, delivered the Gettysburg Address, dedicating the battlefield as a military cemetery.

✴ Admitted West Virginia and Nevada into the Union.

✴ Virginia, Arkansas, North Carolina, and Tennessee seceded from the Union during his presidency. Along with the seven states that left during Buchanan's term, they became the Confederate States of America under President Jefferson Davis. Lincoln spent his entire presidency trying to restore the Union.

Presidential Stats

TERM: 1861–1865

FIRST LADY: Mary Anne Todd Lincoln

VICE PRESIDENT: Hannibal Hamlin (first term), Andrew Johnson (second term)

POLITICAL PARTY: Republican

BORN: February 12, 1809 (Hardin County, Kentucky)

DIED: April 15, 1865 (Washington, DC)

OCCUPATION BEFORE PRESIDENCY: Lawyer, member of the U.S. House of Representatives

NICKNAME: Honest Abe

ANDREW JOHNSON

During the dark days
Of Johnson's impeachment,
He befriended some rodents
While feeling quite cheated.
A family of mice
Lived in his room.
He'd feed them biscuits
As he pondered his doom.
His furry-haired friends
Treated him nice;
Of mice and men,
He would choose mice.

Tell Me More!

* Johnson was the first president to be impeached—that means he broke the law and some people didn't want him to be president anymore! He was charged with replacing the secretary of war without the consent of the Senate. In the end, Congress voted to let him stay and he finished out his term.

* When he was a teenager, Johnson worked as a tailor. He never had any formal education, and he taught himself how to read and write.

* Even though Johnson was a Democrat, he served as vice president to Abraham Lincoln, a Republican.

* Johnson sewed all his own clothes.

Presidential Stats

TERM: 1865–1869

FIRST LADY: Eliza McCardle Johnson

VICE PRESIDENT: None

POLITICAL PARTY: Democrat

BORN: December 29, 1808 (Raleigh, North Carolina)

DIED: July 31, 1875 (Carter County, Tennessee)

OCCUPATION BEFORE PRESIDENCY: Tailor, member of the U.S. House of Representatives and U.S. Senate, vice president of the United States

NICKNAME: The Tennessee Tailor

Accomplishments & Events

* Signed legislation creating the U.S. Department of Education.

* Purchased Alaska from Russia for 7.2 million dollars.

* Passed the 13th and 14th Amendments. These outlawed slavery and gave former slaves citizenship.

* Admitted Nebraska into the Union.

* Readmitted Tennessee, Arkansas, Florida, North Carolina, Louisiana, South Carolina, and Alabama into the Union.

ULYSSES S. GRANT

The Grants owned a dog
And several canaries.
They had horses galore
And found riding quite merry.
One fine cheery day
When it was sunny outside,
In his horse and buggy
Ulysses went for a ride.
He rode around town,
Enjoying the scenery.
He sped along M Street,
Past houses and greenery.
Then a cop pulled him over
For driving too fast.
When he saw who was driving,
He nearly collapsed!

Tell Me More!

✷ The policeman was one of the newest African-American police officers in the city, and he offered to let the president go free. But Grant insisted, "Officer, do your duty." In the end, Grant was charged a fine, his horse was taken away temporarily, and he had to walk back to the White House.

✷ Grant's children had two ponies named Reb and Billy Button. The Grants also had a Newfoundland dog named Faithful and a parrot.

✷ Grant was the first president to run against a woman. Victoria Claflin Woodhull, the leader of the American women's suffrage movement, was a candidate in the 1872 presidential race.

✷ Grant was born Hiram Ulysses Grant. He attended West Point, where he was wrongly enrolled as Ulysses Simpson Grant. Simpson was his mother's middle name, not his. Eventually he accepted Ulysses S. Grant as his real name, but claimed his middle initial didn't stand for anything.

✷ Grant declared Christmas Day a federal holiday.

Presidential Stats

TERM: 1869–1877

FIRST LADY: Julia Boggs Dent Grant

VICE PRESIDENT: Schuyler Colfax (first term), Henry Wilson (second term)

POLITICAL PARTY: Republican

BORN: April 27, 1822 (Point Pleasant, Ohio)

DIED: July 23, 1885 (Mount McGregor, New York)

OCCUPATION BEFORE PRESIDENCY: Commanding general of the United States Army during the Civil War

NICKNAMES: Uncle Sam, Unconditional Surrender

Accomplishments & Events

✷ President during the Panic of 1873, which caused an economic recession during which eighteen thousand businesses failed and unemployment soared to 14 percent.

✷ Enforced civil rights laws and sent troops to fight Ku Klux Klan violence against African-Americans.

✷ Signed the law that established Yellowstone as the first national park.

✷ Admitted Colorado into the Union.

✷ Readmitted Virginia, Georgia, Mississippi, and Texas into the Union.

RUTHERFORD BIRCHARD HAYES

First Lady Lucy
Was sent a small crate
From the city of Bangkok.
It contained a new mate.
A Siamese cat
Was given to her,
The first of its kind
In the U.S. to purr.
The cat made grand entrées
When guests came to call,
And even attended
One or two fancy balls.
They named her Siam.
She lived like a queen:
Went where she wanted,
Ate gourmet cuisine.
Even the dog-loving
President agreed;
Siam was treated
Like royalty, indeed!

Tell Me More!

✻ Historically, Siamese cats were regal pets owned by Siamese royalty. (Siam is now Thailand.)

✻ Hayes also owned a Greyhound dog named Grim, an Elkhound dog named Weejie, and two shepherd dogs named Hector and Nellie. The family also owned Jersey cows, a goat, a mockingbird, kittens, and horses.

✻ Hayes was the first president to have a telephone in the White House.

✻ Lucy Hayes was the first First Lady who had a college degree.

Presidential Stats

TERM: 1877–1881

FIRST LADY: Lucy Ware Webb Hayes

VICE PRESIDENT: William A. Wheeler

POLITICAL PARTY: Republican

BORN: October 4, 1822 (Delaware, Ohio)

DIED: January 17, 1893 (Fremont, Ohio)

OCCUPATION BEFORE PRESIDENCY: Lawyer, member of the U.S. House of Representatives, governor of Ohio

NICKNAME: His Fraudulency

Accomplishments & Events

✻ Signed a bill in February of 1879 that allowed women lawyers to argue cases before the Supreme Court.

✻ Ended Reconstruction in the South by withdrawing federal troops on the condition that the Southern Democrats would allow African-Americans the right to vote.

✻ Vetoed a bill that restricted Chinese immigration into the country. As a compromise, he revised the 1868 Burlingame-Seward Treaty so that it limited, but not completely prohibited, Chinese immigration.

JAMES ABRAM GARFIELD

In Mentor, Ohio,
The Garfields had a home
Where their beloved canine
Would frolic and roam.
The dog's name was Veto;
He was Garfield's favorite friend.
But during his time as president,
A veto was never penned.

Tell Me More!

✸ A veto is when the president rejects a bill passed by the Senate and the House of Representatives. Garfield was the last president who never vetoed a bill.

✸ First Daughter Molly owned a mare named Kit.

✸ Garfield is one of four presidents who was assassinated. On July 2, 1881, Garfield was shot by a man named Charles Guiteau. Guiteau had tried to contact the president several times prior to the shooting, and had dreamed of being a foreign ambassador.

✸ Garfield was the first left-handed president.

✸ Garfield is the only president who was a preacher. During his presidency, he also served as a lay minister at his church.

Presidential Stats

TERM: 1881

FIRST LADY: Lucretia Rudolph Garfield

VICE PRESIDENT: Chester A. Arthur

POLITICAL PARTY: Republican

BORN: November 19, 1831 (Cuyahoga County, Ohio)

DIED: September 19, 1881 (Elberon, New Jersey)

OCCUPATION BEFORE PRESIDENCY: Teacher, preacher, lawyer, member of the U.S. House of Representatives

NICKNAME: Preacher President

Accomplishments & Events

✸ Helped Clara Barton establish the American Red Cross.

✸ Investigated tax fraud that involved postal officials and members of Congress stealing money. This investigation led to civil service reforms.

CHESTER ALAN ARTHUR

As president, Chester Arthur
Did many important things:
Dedicated the Washington Monument
And liaised with foreign kings.
He adorned the White House rooms
With Tiffany stained glass,
And quickly became known
As a man with lots of class.
Many called him Walrus
For his mustache silhouette,
But despite his animal nickname
He did not own any pets.

Tell Me More!

✶ Arthur was probably too busy fishing for salmon to take care of a pet! He was a member of the famous Ristigouche Salmon Club, a private organization comprising the country's most eminent fishermen.

✶ Arthur used to be a lawyer in New York. He once defended a black woman named Lizzie Jennings, who was thrown from a streetcar in Brooklyn because of her race. He won, causing public transportation in New York City to become desegregated.

✶ Arthur owned more than eighty pairs of trousers, and would change his pants several times a day.

✶ Arthur hired stained-glass artist Louis Comfort Tiffany to redecorate the White House's state rooms. To this day many of the original Tiffany pieces still adorn the White House.

Presidential Stats

TERM: 1881–1885

FIRST LADY: Ellen Lewis Herndon Arthur

VICE PRESIDENT: None

POLITICAL PARTY: Republican

BORN: October 5, 1829 (Fairfield, Vermont)

DIED: November 18, 1886 (New York, New York)

OCCUPATION BEFORE PRESIDENCY: Lawyer, teacher, vice president of the United States

NICKNAME: The Gentleman Boss

Accomplishments & Events

✶ Passed the Pendleton Civil Service Reform Act that stated government jobs should be granted based on merit. It also protected employees from being fired or demoted for political reasons.

✶ Passed legislation to keep criminals and mentally ill people from other countries out of the United States.

✶ Signed the Chinese Exclusion Act that put a stop to Chinese immigration for ten years.

GROVER CLEVELAND

As animal lovers,
The Clevelands accrued
So many pets,
Their house was a zoo!
Foxhounds and dachshunds
Ran all around,
Chasing wild rabbits
All over the grounds.
In the side stables,
Horses would graze
While chickens ran free
Every which way.
Grover had daughters,
Esther and Ruth.
There was never a shortage
Of pets for these youths!

Tell Me More!

✳ Cleveland is the only president to serve two terms that weren't back-to-back.

✳ First Lady Frances was twenty-one years old when she married Cleveland. They had their wedding ceremony at the White House.

✳ There was a rat problem in the White House during Cleveland's second term.

✳ Curtiss Candy Company claims they named their Baby Ruth candy bar after Cleveland's daughter Ruth. Others speculate it was named after Babe Ruth, the baseball player.

✳ Cleveland was originally named Stephen Grover Cleveland, but he dropped his first name in early boyhood.

Presidential Stats

TERM: 1885–1889 and 1893–1897

FIRST LADY: Frances Clara Folsom Cleveland

VICE PRESIDENT: Thomas A. Hendricks (first term), Adlai E. Stevenson (second term)

POLITICAL PARTY: Democrat

BORN: March 18, 1837 (Caldwell, New Jersey)

DIED: June 24, 1908 (Princeton, New Jersey)

OCCUPATION BEFORE PRESIDENCY: Lawyer, sheriff, mayor of Buffalo, NY, governor of New York

NICKNAME: Uncle Jumbo

Accomplishments & Events

✳ During his first term, passed the Interstate Commerce Act. This act created the Interstate Commerce Commission that regulated railroad rates.

✳ During his second term, the country fell into a financial depression known as the Panic of 1893. Thousands of businesses failed and riots broke out all over the country.

✳ During his second term, admitted Utah into the Union.

BENJAMIN HARRISON IV

Benjamin's goat, Whiskers,
Ran off one day,
Dragging his grandkids
Behind in a sleigh.
He ran 'cross the lawn
And then through the gate.
The president ran after them,
Growing irate.
The next day's newspapers
Spread the word around town
About the runaway president
And the goat he chased down.

Tell Me More!

✺ None of Harrison's grandchildren were harmed during the goat chase!

✺ Harrison's grandfather William Henry Harrison was the ninth president of the United States. They both had goats named Whiskers at the White House (Benjamin's was Old Whiskers, and his grandfather's was His Whiskers).

✺ First Lady Caroline owned a collie dog named Dash, who had his own doghouse on the White House grounds.

✺ During Harrison's term, electricity was installed in the White House.

Presidential Stats

TERM: 1889–1893

FIRST LADY: Caroline Lavinia Scott Harrison

VICE PRESIDENT: Levi P. Morton

POLITICAL PARTY: Republican

BORN: August 20, 1833 (North Bend, Ohio)

DIED: March 13, 1901 (Indianapolis, Indiana)

OCCUPATION BEFORE PRESIDENCY: Lawyer, Supreme Court reporter, member of the U.S. Senate

NICKNAME: Little Ben

Accomplishments & Events

✺ Ordered the American flag to be flown over the White House and all government buildings. He also urged public buildings and schools to do the same.

✺ Signed the Sherman Anti-Trust Act that regulated the activities of corporations to prevent monopolies and trusts from forming.

✺ Admitted North Dakota, South Dakota, Montana, Washington, Idaho, and Wyoming into the Union.

WILLIAM McKINLEY, JR.

William had a parrot;
Washington Post was its name.
It had a yellow head
And from Mexico it came.
Will would often whistle
As he strolled along;
His parrot whistled back
And finished up his song.

Presidential Stats

TERM: 1897–1901

FIRST LADY: Ida Saxton McKinley

VICE PRESIDENT: Garret A. Hobart (first term),
Theodore Roosevelt (second term)

POLITICAL PARTY: Republican

BORN: January 29, 1843 (Niles, Ohio)

DIED: September 14, 1901 (Buffalo, New York)

OCCUPATION BEFORE PRESIDENCY: Lawyer, county
prosecutor, member of the U.S. House of Representatives,
governor of Ohio

NICKNAME: Idol of Ohio

Tell Me More!

✶ McKinley and Washington Post's favorite duet was
"Yankee Doodle."

✶ The McKinleys also owned two angora kittens named
Enrique DeLome (after the Spanish ambassador) and
Valeriano Weyler (after the governor of Cuba).

✶ In 1901, McKinley was assassinated in Buffalo, NY.
The shooter was an out-of-work mill worker who saw
politicians as a threat to the working-class community.

✶ McKinley always wore a red carnation in his lapel
for good luck. After he died, Ohio made it their state
flower in his honor.

Accomplishments & Events

✶ The Spanish-American war began after the U.S.
Battleship *Maine* blew up in the Havana harbor.
McKinley did not want to enter a war with Spain,
but he felt pressured by the Democratic Party to take
action.

✶ When America won the two-year war, it gained
temporary control of Cuba and permanent authority
over Puerto Rico, Guam, and the Philippines.
McKinley questioned whether the Constitution would
apply to these territories, but later agreed with Congress
that because they were outside of the free trade area,
they would not be subject to Constitutional provisions.

✶ Signed the Gold Standard Act, establishing gold as the
only standard for paper money.

THEODORE ROOSEVELT, JR.

The Roosevelts owned
Snakes, pigs, and cats,
A hyena, a lion,
A zebra, some rats.
There was Josiah the badger,
Who could be quite mean.
And First Daughter Alice
Had a snake that was green.
But it was Teddy's own dog
Who caused a big stir
That threatened the safety
Of a certain monsieur.
Teddy's dog Pete
Often nipped at his guests;
A cabinet member
Once got bit in the chest.
But one day the terrier
Bit off the pants
Of Jules Jusserand,
The Ambassador of France!
Despite how he felt,
There was no other solution
Than to send Pete away
Or risk a French revolution.

Tell Me More!

✴ Teddy bears are rumored to have been invented when Roosevelt refused to shoot a small bear cub one day, which inspired a toy company to come out with the cute stuffed "teddy" bears.

✴ Alice's garter snake was named Emily Spinach "because it was as green as spinach and as thin as my Aunt Emily."

✴ The Roosevelts had more than forty pets living at the White House. Favorites included Eli Yale (Quentin Roosevelt's macaw parrot), Jack (Kermit Roosevelt's terrier), Algonquin (Quentin Roosevelt's pony), and Manchu (Alice Roosevelt's Pekingese dog). They also owned guinea pigs, a one-legged rooster, a raccoon, and bears!

✴ Roosevelt is the only president to receive a Congressional Medal of Honor (for his heroic actions during the Spanish-American War). He also won the Nobel Peace Prize for his work ending the Russo-Japanese War.

Presidential Stats

TERM: 1901–1909

FIRST LADY: Edith Kermit Carow Roosevelt

VICE PRESIDENT: Charles W. Fairbanks

POLITICAL PARTY: Republican

BORN: October 27, 1858 (New York, New York)

DIED: January 6, 1919 (Oyster Bay, New York)

OCCUPATION BEFORE PRESIDENCY: President of the New York City Police Board, assistant secretary of the Navy, governor of New York, vice president of the United States

NICKNAMES: TR, Trust-Buster, Teddy

Accomplishments & Events

✴ Oversaw the construction of the Panama Canal.

✴ Prosecuted several corporations for violating the Sherman Anti-Trust Act, earning him the nickname Trust-Buster.

✴ Signed both the Pure Food and Drug Act and the Meat Inspection Act. These allowed for government inspection of meat, and required all medicines and drugs to be labeled with ingredients and dosage information.

✴ Doubled the number of national parks in the country.

✴ Admitted Oklahoma into the Union.

WILLIAM HOWARD TAFT

William Taft
Had a problem with weight.
Whenever near food,
He ate and he ate!
His weakness was milk,
But he could not abstain
For it came from his cow,
Miss Pauline Wayne.
He'd drink ten glasses
Every day before noon,
And his waist would expand
Like a giant balloon!

Tell Me More!

✳ Pauline Wayne was the president's second cow at the White House, replacing his first cow, Mooly Wolly. Miss Wayne, as she was often called, was the last cow to live at the White House.

✳ One day while bathing in his bathtub, Taft got stuck. It took four men and a gallon of lard to get the president out.

✳ First Lady Helen arranged for the planting of the three thousand Japanese cherry trees that grace the Washington Tidal Basin.

✳ Taft was the first president to throw a baseball at the first game of the season. The tradition continues today.

Presidential Stats

TERM: 1909–1913

FIRST LADY: Helen Louise Herron Taft

VICE PRESIDENT: James S. Sherman

POLITICAL PARTY: Republican

BORN: September 15, 1857 (Cincinnati, Ohio)

DIED: March 8, 1930 (Washington, DC)

OCCUPATION BEFORE PRESIDENCY: Lawyer, tax collector, governor of the Philippines, secretary of war

NICKNAME: Big Bill

Accomplishments & Events

✳ Passed the 16th Amendment that required citizens to pay income tax.

✳ Like Roosevelt, prosecuted big trust corporations. He won victories against the American Tobacco Company and the Standard Oil Company.

✳ Admitted New Mexico and Arizona into the Union.

WOODROW WILSON

Woodrow had a flock of sheep;
On the back lawn they grazed.
All their wool was auctioned off,
And fifty grand was raised.
It was given to the Red Cross
To help out with the war.
They cared for wounded soldiers,
Built hospitals, and more.

Tell Me More!

✳ The Wilsons had a ram named Old Ike.

✳ During World War I, the Wilsons stopped entertaining at the White House. First Lady Edith established meatless, heatless, and gasless days.

✳ Originally named Thomas Woodrow Wilson, he dropped his first name after graduating from college.

✳ Wilson was awarded the Nobel Peace Prize for his work establishing the League of Nations.

✳ First Lady Edith Wilson was a descendant of Pocahontas.

Presidential Stats

TERM: 1913–1921

FIRST LADY: Ellen Louise Axson Wilson and Edith Bolling Galt Wilson

VICE PRESIDENT: Thomas R. Marshall

POLITICAL PARTY: Democrat

BORN: December 28, 1856 (Staunton, Virginia)

DIED: February 3, 1924 (Washington, DC)

OCCUPATION BEFORE PRESIDENCY: College professor, president of Princeton University, governor of New Jersey

NICKNAME: Schoolmaster of Politics

Accomplishments & Events

✳ Presided over the country during World War I.

✳ Passed the 17th Amendment (allowing citizens to elect U.S. Senators), 18th Amendment (prohibiting alcoholic beverages), and the 19th Amendment (giving women the right to vote).

✳ Signed the Federal Reserve Act that created the Federal Reserve System, the government's central banking system.

✳ Established the National Park Service.

WARREN GAMALIEL HARDING

Harding had Laddie Boy,
A beloved Airedale dog.
If Laddie were around today,
He'd probably have a blog!
Newspapers wrote about
The First Pup's affairs;
At cabinet meetings,
Laddie had his own chair.
He even hosted the best
Easter Egg Roll yet!
Yes, Laddie was the country's
First celebrity pet.

Tell Me More!

✷ When Harding died in 1923, newsboys all over the country collected more than nineteen thousand pennies that were melted and sculpted into a statue of Laddie Boy. Harding had worked in the newspaper business before becoming president.

✷ The Hardings also had a bulldog named Oh Boy. First Lady Florence kept canaries at the White House.

✷ Harding had a squirrel named Pete who lived on the White House grounds.

✷ Harding was the first president to win an election in which women could vote.

Presidential Stats

TERM: 1921–1923

FIRST LADY: Florence Mabel Kling DeWolfe Harding

VICE PRESIDENT: Calvin Coolidge

POLITICAL PARTY: Republican

BORN: November 2, 1865 (Caledonia—now Blooming Grove—Ohio)

DIED: August 2, 1923 (San Francisco, California)

OCCUPATION BEFORE PRESIDENCY: Insurance salesman, newspaper publisher, member of the U.S. Senate

NICKNAME: Wobbly Warren

Accomplishments & Events

✷ Signed the treaty that ended World War I.

✷ Established tax cuts in order to boost the postwar economy.

✷ Established the Bureau of the Budget that placed restrictions on government spending.

CALVIN COOLIDGE, JR.

Amongst all the dogs,
The cats, and the birds
Was Rebecca the raccoon,
A pet quite absurd.
Originally a present
For a Thanksgiving feast,
The Coolidges felt
She was too cute to eat.
So they took her in
And gave her a home.
Through the White House halls
She'd scamper and roam.
The staff, however,
Did not find her funny,
For she would rip clothing
And sometimes steal money!
But when she got loose
And ran through the gate,
The First Family feared
For their furry friend's fate.
So sadly they had
To bid her adieu,
And sent her to safety
At the National Zoo.

Tell Me More!

* While most Americans dined on simple food, Rebecca was fed green shrimp, chicken, eggs (her favorite), and expensive cream.
* The Coolidges also had two kittens named Tiger and Blackie. Calvin enjoyed walking about the White House with Tiger draped around his neck.
* The Coolidges had more than twenty-five pets, including ten dogs, a goose, an antelope, a donkey, a bobcat, a lion, bears, a hippo, and a wallaby.
* Coolidge's favorite dog was a white collie named Rob Roy. A portrait of Rob Roy with First Lady Grace still hangs in the White House today.
* Born John Calvin Coolidge, Jr., he dropped his first name in boyhood.

Presidential Stats

TERM: 1923–1929

FIRST LADY: Grace Anna Goodhue Coolidge

VICE PRESIDENT: Charles G. Dawes

POLITICAL PARTY: Republican

BORN: July 4, 1872 (Plymouth, Vermont)

DIED: January 5, 1933 (Northampton, Massachusetts)

OCCUPATION BEFORE PRESIDENCY: Lawyer, governor of Massachusetts, vice president of the United States

NICKNAME: Silent Cal

Accomplishments & Events

* Limited the country's federal spending and reduced the taxes that were enforced during World War I.
* During Coolidge's presidency, Charles Lindbergh made his famous solo flight across the Atlantic Ocean in the *Spirit of St. Louis*. When Lindbergh returned to the United States, the president welcomed him home in a ceremony held at the Washington Monument.
* Signed the Immigration Act of 1924 that limited the number of immigrants allowed into the country. It prevented Japanese citizens from gaining citizenship, and instead favored northern Europeans.

HERBERT CLARK HOOVER

First Son Allan Henry
Owned two uncommon pets
That roamed through the grounds
And made some staff upset.
Blame John Quincy Adams
For making it okay
To have gators at the White House,
Wandering astray!

Tell Me More!

- In addition to the alligators, the Hoovers owned several dogs. Herbert's favorite was his German shepherd King Tut.
- Hoover was orphaned as a child and became a self-made millionaire as a mining engineer. As president, he refused his salary.
- Hoover's vice president, Charles Curtis, is the only nonwhite vice president to date. Curtis was part Kaw Indian.
- Hoover spoke fluent Chinese.

Presidential Stats

TERM: 1929–1933
FIRST LADY: Lou Henry Hoover
VICE PRESIDENT: Charles Curtis
POLITICAL PARTY: Republican
BORN: August 10, 1874 (West Branch, Iowa)
DIED: October 20, 1964 (New York, New York)
OCCUPATION BEFORE PRESIDENCY: Mining engineer, secretary of commerce
NICKNAME: The Great Engineer

Accomplishments & Events

- On October 29, 1929, the stock market crashed and the Great Depression began. By 1930, four million Americans were unemployed, and that number tripled by 1933. To make up for lost revenue, Hoover greatly increased income, estate, and corporate taxes.
- Signed the Agricultural Marketing Act that tried to provide financial relief to farmers. In the end, the financial losses were too great to manage.
- Passed the 20th Amendment that moved the presidential inauguration up from March 4 to January 20.

FRANKLIN DELANO ROOSEVELT

Franklin's dog Fala
Tagged alongside
The president wherever
He traveled worldwide.
They went on a trip
To the Aleutian Islands
(Which are located southwest
Of the Alaskan highlands).
After they returned
A lie circulated
That the Republican Party
Seemed to have created.
The rumor said Fala
Had been forgotten
Back on the islands,
Making Franklin feel rotten.
They said a warship
Was sent in a dash,
Costing millions of dollars
Of taxpayers' cash.
Franklin went on
The news to address
This lie that was started
And picked up by the press.
He talked about how
The accusations were spurious
And said Fala himself
Was really quite furious!

Tell Me More!

✻ Fala starred in an MGM movie and was also an honorary private in the United States Army. Each year, he received thousands of letters from fans around the world.

✻ Fala was once rushed to the hospital with a severe intestinal problem because the staff was feeding him too much. Afterward, Roosevelt declared he was the only person allowed to feed Fala.

✻ The Roosevelts also owned several other dogs, including a German shepherd named Major, an English sheepdog named Tiny, and a Llewellyn setter named Winks.

✻ Roosevelt contracted polio when he was thirty-nine years old and was paralyzed from the waist down. Through rigorous exercise he learned to stand with braces.

✻ Roosevelt is the only president to serve more than two terms. He suffered a stroke at the start of his fourth term and died soon after.

Presidential Stats

TERM: 1933–1945

FIRST LADY: Anna Eleanor Roosevelt

VICE PRESIDENT: John N. Garner (first and second terms), Henry A. Wallace (third term), Harry S. Truman (fourth term)

POLITICAL PARTY: Democrat

BORN: January 30, 1882 (Hyde Park, New York)

DIED: April 12, 1945 (Warm Springs, Georgia)

OCCUPATION BEFORE PRESIDENCY: Lawyer, assistant secretary of the Navy, governor of New York

NICKNAME: FDR

Accomplishments & Events

✻ To end the Great Depression, developed the New Deal, which created jobs for the poor, established the National Recovery Administration, and included the National Housing Act and the Social Security Act.

✻ Passed the 21st Amendment in 1933, putting an end to prohibition and allowing alcoholic beverages to be sold.

✻ Asked Congress for a Declaration of War with Japan after the Japanese attacked Pearl Harbor on December 7, 1941, and presided over the country during World War II.

✻ On June 6, 1944, General Eisenhower landed at Normandy. Known as D-day, this led to the liberation of Paris and the end of World War II. That same evening, the president went on the radio and read a prayer he had written for the nation.

✻ Founded the National Foundation for Infantile Paralysis, which later became the March of Dimes.

HARRY S. TRUMAN

Then, of course,
There was Harry Truman,
Who wasn't really
A dog-loving human.
But one winter day
A small package arrived
With a tiny blond
Cocker spaniel inside.
The puppy came tagged
With the name Feller,
But Truman didn't want
A new White House dweller.
He tried to give Feller
To the family physician,
But the story appeared
In the morning edition.
The entire nation
Was soon up in arms;
An anti-dog president
Was cause for alarm!
To quiet the presses,
The president planned
To send him to the Navy
At a base in Maryland.
From there the media
Stayed far away,
And several soldiers
Took care of the stray.

Tell Me More!

✴ Feller was sent to Camp David (which was then called Shangri-La). Located about sixty miles northwest of Washington, DC, Camp David is a presidential retreat and a U.S. Navy installation. It is staffed heavily by the U.S. Navy and the U.S. Marine Corps, and is known as one of the most secure locations in the world.

✴ As a boy, Truman played the piano. He used to wake up at five o'clock every morning and practice for two hours.

✴ Truman was the first president to give a speech on television.

✴ Truman didn't have a middle name, only a middle initial.

Presidential Stats

TERM: 1945–1953
FIRST LADY: Elizabeth (Bess) Virginia Wallace Truman
VICE PRESIDENT: Alben W. Barkley
POLITICAL PARTY: Democrat
BORN: May 8, 1884 (Lamar, Missouri)
DIED: December 26, 1972 (Kansas City, Missouri)
OCCUPATION BEFORE PRESIDENCY: Bank clerk, farmer, member of the U.S. Senate, vice president of the United States
NICKNAME: Give 'Em Hell Harry

Accomplishments & Events

✴ Supervised the conclusion of World War II. He ordered the atomic bomb attack on Hiroshima and demanded Japanese surrender.

✴ Helped create the United Nations, an international organization committed to maintaining peace between nations.

✴ Sent U.S. troops to aid South Korea in the Korean War conflict.

✴ Passed the 22nd Amendment, which allows presidents to serve no more than two terms.

DWIGHT DAVID EISENHOWER

A gray dog named Heidi
Was Dwight's favorite pet.
She'd tag alongside him
Wherever he went.
But First Lady Mamie
Did not get along
With Dwight's furry friend;
Their dislike was strong.
One day the First Lady
Punished the pup
And sent her away;
She'd had quite enough!
Heidi left the room
Feeling quite smug
And pooped
On a very expensive rug!

Tell Me More!

✳ After ruining the rug (it was worth $20,000!), Heidi was sent to live at the Eisenhowers' farm in Gettysburg. She later gave birth to two puppies.

✳ The Eisenhowers' grandchildren had a little Scottie dog named Skunky who would go with them when they visited the White House.

✳ Eisenhower served in both World War I and World War II. He was in charge of the D-day Invasion of France during World War II.

✳ Eisenhower signed a bill that added the words "under God" in the Pledge of Allegiance.

Presidential Stats

TERM: 1953–1961

FIRST LADY: Mamie Geneva Doud Eisenhower

VICE PRESIDENT: Richard M. Nixon

POLITICAL PARTY: Republican

BORN: October 14, 1890 (Denison, Texas)

DIED: March 28, 1969 (Washington, DC)

OCCUPATION BEFORE PRESIDENCY: Five-star general of the Army, president of Columbia University, supreme commander of the North Atlantic Treaty Organization

NICKNAME: Ike

Accomplishments & Events

✳ Oversaw the end of the Korean War conflict.

✳ Signed the Civil Rights Act of 1960.

✳ Integrated the public school system and made public facilities in Washington, DC, available to all races.

✳ Admitted Alaska and Hawaii into the Union.

JOHN FITZGERALD KENNEDY

A present was given
To First Daughter Caroline
From the Soviet prime minister
As a diplomatic sign:
A mongrel pup, Pushinka,
Who had a furry face.
Her momma was Strelka,
One of the first dogs in space.
Within the White House walls
She gave birth to four pups
Who appeared with JFK
In many photo ops.
They were Blackie, Butterfly,
Streaker, and White Tips,
But JFK referred to them
As his very own pupniks!

Presidential Stats

TERM: 1961–1963
FIRST LADY: Jacqueline Lee Bouvier Kennedy
VICE PRESIDENT: Lyndon B. Johnson
POLITICAL PARTY: Democrat
BORN: May 29, 1917 (Brookline, Massachusetts)
DIED: November 22, 1963 (Dallas, Texas)
OCCUPATION BEFORE PRESIDENCY: Journalist, member of the U.S. House of Representatives and the U.S. Senate
NICKNAME: JFK

Tell Me More!

✳ Caroline Kennedy had a pony named Macaroni, who roamed freely around the White House. Macaroni received fan mail from all over the world.

✳ First Lady Jacqueline Kennedy owned a horse named Sardar, a gift from President Ayub Khan of Pakistan. "Sardar" in Persian means "leader."

✳ The Kennedys had more than twenty pets in all. They owned several horses, a cat named Tom Kitten, a canary named Robin, parakeets named Bluebell and Maybelle, hamsters named Debbie and Billie, and a rabbit named Zsa Zsa.

✳ In 1961, Kennedy's nephew Robert Kennedy, Jr., gave a spotted salamander to the president.

✳ On November 22, 1963, Kennedy was shot in Dallas, Texas, while on his way to deliver a speech. Dignitaries from more than ninety countries attended his funeral.

Accomplishments & Events

✳ Peacefully defused the Cuban Missile Crisis (thirteen days in October 1962 when the Soviets placed nuclear missiles in Cuba).

✳ Founded the Peace Corps, sending young Americans to do humanitarian work in developing countries.

✳ During his presidency, the Berlin Wall was built by the Soviets. The Wall divided East and West Germany. In the summer of 1963, Kennedy visited Berlin and gave one of his most memorable speeches. Shortly after his death, the square where he spoke was renamed John F. Kennedy Platz.

✳ On August 28, 1963, Dr. Martin Luther King, Jr., gave his "I Have a Dream" speech at the March on Washington. King's speech put pressure on the Kennedy administration to advance civil rights legislation in Congress.

Johnson's dog Him
Was one of his beagles.
He lived at the White House
And was treated quite regal.
Some dogs like toys,
Others like to be hugged,
But the truth is Him liked
To have his ears tugged!

Tell Me More!

✳ A photo was printed in *TIME* magazine that showed the president tugging on Him's ears. Johnson had to go on national news and apologize for treating his dog in such a manner. But the truth is Him enjoyed having his ears pulled.

✳ Him had a sister named Her. Both of the dogs appeared on the cover of *Life* magazine on June 19, 1964. Johnson also owned several more beagles. There was Beagle, Little Beagle, and J. Edgar. He also owned a white collie named Blanco.

✳ Johnson also had a mongrel dog named Yuki, who was found at a Texas gas station by Johnson's daughter Luci. Johnson and Yuki would "sing" together in the Oval Office.

✳ The Johnsons owned lovebirds and hamsters.

✳ Johnson was the first president to nominate an African-American (Thurgood Marshall) for the Supreme Court.

Presidential Stats

TERM: 1963–1969

FIRST LADY: Claudia Alta (Lady Bird) Taylor Johnson

VICE PRESIDENT: Hubert H. Humphrey

POLITICAL PARTY: Democrat

BORN: August 27, 1908 (Stonewall, Texas)

DIED: January 22, 1973 (Stonewall, Texas)

OCCUPATION BEFORE PRESIDENCY: Teacher, member of the U.S. House of Representatives and the U.S. Senate, vice president of the United States

NICKNAME: LBJ

Accomplishments & Events

✳ Established Medicare, giving the elderly low-cost medical insurance.

✳ Established Medicaid, giving medical insurance to the poor.

✳ During his presidency, Dr. Martin Luther King, Jr., and Robert F. Kennedy (John F. Kennedy's brother) were both assassinated. In response, Johnson signed the Gun Control Act of 1968, one of the biggest federal gun control laws in American history.

✳ Signed civil rights legislation that banned discrimination in the workplace and public places like hotels and restaurants.

RICHARD MILHOUS NIXON

When Nixon was campaigning,
A story came out
That he received gifts
In his own bank account.
Nixon did admit
To accepting a present:
Not money or a car,
But a canine resident!
A baby cocker spaniel
From a Texas devotee
Was the newest member
Of the Nixon family.
This little human glimpse
Truly rocked the boat,
Causing Nixon to earn
The American people's vote.

Presidential Stats

TERM: 1969–1974

FIRST LADY: Thelma Catherine (Pat) Ryan Nixon

VICE PRESIDENT: Spiro Agnew (first term); Gerald Ford (second term)

POLITICAL PARTY: Republican

BORN: January 9, 1913 (Yorba Linda, California)

DIED: April 22, 1994 (New York, New York)

OCCUPATION BEFORE PRESIDENCY: Lawyer, member of the U.S. House of Representatives and the U.S. Senate, vice president of the United States

NICKNAME: Tricky Dick

Tell Me More!

* The Nixons named the puppy Checkers because he was black and white like a checkerboard. They were given Checkers during Nixon's campaign for the vice presidency (he was Eisenhower's running mate).

* First Daughter Julie had a French poodle named Vicky, and First Daughter Trisha owned a Yorkshire terrier named Pasha. Nixon also had an Irish setter named King Timahoe.

* Nixon was the first president to keep pet fish at the White House.

* Nixon was found guilty of lying to the Senate about his involvement in the Watergate scandal. Nixon quit his job as president before he could be impeached.

* The White House used to have a swimming pool until Nixon filled it with concrete so the press would have more room.

Accomplishments & Events

* Withdrew troops from Vietnam, ending America's involvement in the war.

* Signed the Chemical Weapons Treaty with the Soviet Union that required both countries to destroy all biological and chemical weapons and banned them from making more.

* On July 20, 1969, astronauts Buzz Aldrin and Neil Armstrong landed on the moon. They spoke with Nixon by phone, in what Nixon described as "the most historic phone call ever made from the White House."

* Passed the 26th Amendment, which lowered the voting age from twenty-one to eighteen.

GERALD RUDOLPH FORD, JR.

First Daughter Susan
Came up with a plan
To get a dog for her dad,
A dog-loving man.
She called up a kennel
And said she could spend
The money to buy
A dog for a friend.
The owner said, "Great!
Now what's your friend's name?"
"It's a secret. I can't tell you,"
Susan proclaimed.
"I'm sorry, we don't
Sell dogs that way.
We need to make sure
The dog's home is okay."
"They live in a house.
It's white with a fence."
The owner responded,
"Do they own it or rent?"
Feeling quite cornered,
She could no longer hide
The identity of where
The dog would reside.

Tell Me More!

✴ The dog, a golden retriever, moved to the White House and Ford named her Liberty. Liberty gave birth to a litter of puppies in September 1975.

✴ One night, Ford took Liberty out late at night for a bathroom break and forgot to tell the Secret Service. They both got locked out of the White House and had to bang on a stairwell door until guards heard and let them back in.

✴ First Daughter Susan also had a miniature seal point Siamese cat named Shan.

✴ Ford turned down offers to play for the Green Bay Packers and the Detroit Lions, and instead went into politics.

✴ During his presidency, there were two assassination attempts on Ford's life. Both attempts were by women.

✴ Ford was born Leslie Lynch King, Jr., but changed his name after his mother remarried.

Presidential Stats

TERM: 1974–1977

FIRST LADY: Elizabeth (Betty) Ann Bloomer Warren Ford

VICE PRESIDENT: Nelson A. Rockefeller

POLITICAL PARTY: Republican

BORN: July 14, 1913 (Omaha, Nebraska)

DIED: December 26, 2006 (Rancho Mirage, California)

OCCUPATION BEFORE PRESIDENCY: Lawyer, member of the U.S. House of Representatives, House minority leader, vice president of the United States

NICKNAMES: Jerry, Mr. Nice Guy

Accomplishments & Events

✴ Granted former President Nixon a pardon for his involvement in the Watergate scandal.

✴ Reduced inflation by more than half.

✴ Offered an amnesty program to Vietnam draft dodgers that gave them lenient punishments instead of jail time.

JAMES EARL CARTER, JR.

Daughter Amy roller-skated
Through the White House rooms.
Past the Oval Office
She would zip and zoom!
She even built a tree house
On the estate's backyard
And held many sleepovers
With Secret Service standing guard.
But her favorite White House pastime
Was to snuggle in her chair
And stroke her Siamese cat
Misty Malarky Ying Yang's hair.
Sadly, Jimmy was too busy
To have his very own pet,
For the Iran hostage crisis
Had proven quite a threat.

Presidential Stats

TERM: 1977–1981

FIRST LADY: Eleanor Rosalynn Smith Carter

VICE PRESIDENT: Walter F. Mondale

POLITICAL PARTY: Democrat

BORN: October 1, 1924 (Plains, Georgia)

OCCUPATION BEFORE PRESIDENCY: Peanut farmer, governor of Georgia

NICKNAME: Jimmy

Tell Me More!

✳ First Daughter Amy was also given an elephant by a Sri Lankan immigrant. The elephant went to live at the National Zoo.

✳ While on a fishing trip, Carter's boat was followed by a swamp rabbit that he tried to shoo away with an oar. *The Washington Post* ran a photo on the front page with the headline "President Attacked by Rabbit."

✳ Before he was president, Carter ran his family's peanut farm in Plains, Georgia.

✳ Carter won the Nobel Peace Prize in 2002 for his humanitarian work around the world. His organization, the Carter Center, continues to help people.

Accomplishments & Events

✳ Pardoned ten thousand people who dodged the Vietnam War draft.

✳ Created the Department of Energy.

✳ During his presidency, the U.S. Embassy in Teheran, Iran, was seized and the Iranians took over sixty Americans hostage. Carter immediately applied pressure on Iran for the release of the hostages.

RONALD WILSON REAGAN

Prime Minister Margaret
Thatcher
Was visiting DC
And Ronald walked beside her
As they talked policy,
When suddenly First Dog Lucky
Jumped out of a bush,
Ran after the president,
And bit him on his tush!

Tell Me More!

* The Reagans had several different dogs while in the White House. Rex, their Cavalier King Charles spaniel, was often photographed with First Lady Nancy.

* During Reagan's terms, Jelly Belly jelly beans were served in the Oval Office and on Air Force One. "You can tell a lot about a fella's character by whether he picks out all of one color or just grabs a handful," the president would say.

* Before he was president, Reagan was a Hollywood actor. He acted in more than fifty movies, including *Dark Victory* starring Bette Davis and *Santa Fe Trail* with Errol Flynn.

* On March 30, 1981, after finishing a speech, a mentally unstable man named John Hinckley, Jr., shot Reagan in the chest. The president survived the assassination attempt.

Presidential Stats

TERM: 1981–1989

FIRST LADY: Nancy Davis Reagan

VICE PRESIDENT: George H. W. Bush

POLITICAL PARTY: Republican

BORN: February 6, 1911 (Tampico, Illinois)

DIED: June 5, 2004 (Los Angeles, California)

OCCUPATION BEFORE PRESIDENCY: Actor, governor of California

NICKNAMES: The Gipper, The Great Communicator

Accomplishments & Events

* Nominated the first woman (Sandra Day O'Connor) to the Supreme Court.

* Accused of selling weapons to Iran in exchange for the release of American hostages. This scandal was known as the Iran-Contra Affair.

* Signed the U.S.-Canadian Free Trade Agreement that allowed for free trade between the two countries.

* Famously challenged Soviet leader Mikhail Gorbachev to "tear down this wall!" in a speech referring to the Berlin Wall.

GEORGE HERBERT WALKER BUSH

The Bushes' spaniel Millie
Lived a happy life indeed.
She'd frolic in the yard
And come and go with ease.
But then her belly grew;
She was going to be a mom.
She stayed in bed for weeks
Where she was nice and calm.
Soon the day arrived
And Millie birthed her young.
Six new puppies joined the crew,
Five daughters and one son.

Presidential Stats

TERM: 1989–1993

FIRST LADY: Barbara Pierce Bush

VICE PRESIDENT: James Danforth Quayle

POLITICAL PARTY: Republican

BORN: June 12, 1924 (Milton, Massachusetts)

OCCUPATION BEFORE PRESIDENCY: President/CEO of an oil drilling company, member of the U.S. House of Representatives, ambassador to the United Nations, chief liaison to China, director of the Central Intelligence Agency, vice president of the United States

NICKNAME: Poppy

Tell Me More!

✷ Millie and the puppies appeared on the cover of *Life* magazine.

✷ *The Washingtonian* called Millie "The Ugliest Dog," which caused an uproar in Washington. Even Senator Bob Dole spoke out in support of Millie. The magazine apologized and sent Millie some treats.

✷ Millie and First Lady Barbara wrote *Millie's Book*, which became a quick best seller.

✷ Like John Adams, Bush was the father of another president (George W. Bush).

Accomplishments & Events

✷ Met with Mikhail Gorbachev after the fall of Communism and was assured that the Soviet Union would not use nuclear weapons against the United States.

✷ Launched a mission against the Iraqi army called Operation Desert Storm after Iraq invaded Kuwait. This resulted in the Gulf War.

✷ Signed the Americans with Disabilities Act that requires businesses and public organizations to make their facilities wheelchair accessible.

WILLIAM JEFFERSON CLINTON

The Clintons' cat, Socks,
Was treated like a king.
He roamed around the gardens,
Visitor's office, and West Wing.
But when Bill adopted Buddy,
A chocolate Labrador,
From the get-go, he and Socks
Had quite a bad rapport.
Bill was very sad
That peace just never grew:
"I've done better with Palestinians
And Israelis than these two!"

Tell Me More!

⁕ Whenever the two pets were in the same room, Socks would hiss and arch his back. If Buddy refused to leave, Socks would sometimes attack the poor dog.

⁕ Socks was adopted by the family in 1991. First Daughter Chelsea was leaving her weekly piano lesson in Little Rock, Arkansas, when Socks jumped right into her arms. She took him home with her.

⁕ First Lady Hillary served as secretary of state in the Obama administration from 2009 to 2013.

⁕ Originally named William Jefferson Blythe III, he legally changed his last name to Clinton after his mother remarried.

⁕ Clinton is the only president to play the saxophone.

Presidential Stats

TERM: 1993–2001

FIRST LADY: Hillary Diane Rodham Clinton

VICE PRESIDENT: Albert A. Gore, Jr.

POLITICAL PARTY: Democrat

BORN: August 19, 1946 (Hope, Arkansas)

OCCUPATION BEFORE PRESIDENCY: Law professor, attorney general of Arkansas, governor of Arkansas

NICKNAME: Bubba

Accomplishments & Events

⁕ Mediated peaceful agreements between Palestine and Israel. These agreements are often referred to as the Oslo Accords.

⁕ Signed the Brady Handgun Violence Prevention Act that required background checks on people buying guns in the United States.

⁕ Sent U.S. troops to Bosnia to protect the citizens from the Serbian government.

⁕ On April 19, 1995, the Alfred R. Murrah Federal Building in Oklahoma City was bombed. One hundred and sixty-eight people were killed in the attack. Later that day, Clinton declared a federal emergency in Oklahoma City.

GEORGE WALKER BUSH

The Bushes had Scot terriers
Of noble pedigree.
They quickly rose to fame
When they lived within DC.
But one of them named Barney
Caused a big to-do:
When he bit a Reuters journalist,
It aired on the nightly news!
Some asked if he was sick
Of all the media attention,
Or just afraid the Democrats
Would win the next election.

Presidential Stats

TERM: 2001–2009

FIRST LADY: Laura Lane Welch Bush

VICE PRESIDENT: Richard B. Cheney

POLITICAL PARTY: Republican

BORN: July 6, 1946 (New Haven, Connecticut)

OCCUPATION BEFORE PRESIDENCY: Oil businessman, baseball team owner (Texas Rangers), governor of Texas

NICKNAME: Dubya

Tell Me More!

✴ The Bushes' two Scottish terriers were named Barney and Miss Beazley. They starred together in several short movies that aired on the White House's website.

✴ The Bushes also had a Springer spaniel named Spot. Spot was born at the White House to George's parents' dog Millie. She is the only pet to live in the White House during two nonconsecutive terms.

✴ A black cat named India "Willie" Bush also lived with the Bush family at the White House. They named her after Rubén "El Indio" Sierra, a baseball star who played for the Texas Rangers.

✴ Many longhorn cattle live at the Bush family ranch in Crawford, Texas.

✴ Bush is the only president who has fathered twins (daughters Barbara and Jenna Bush).

Accomplishments & Events

✴ During his presidency, Al-Qaeda terrorists attacked the United States on September 11, 2001. In response, President Bush declared a global War on Terror and invaded Afghanistan that same year.

✴ Ordered a military invasion of Iraq in 2003, and the Iraq War began.

✴ Established the President's Emergency Plan for AIDS Relief to fight the HIV/AIDS pandemic in Africa and around the world.

✴ In August of 2005, Hurricane Katrina hit the Gulf coast, causing the city of New Orleans to become flooded. Two days before the hurricane reached land, Bush declared a state of emergency in areas of Louisiana, Alabama, and Mississippi.

BARACK HUSSEIN OBAMA II

The First Daughters were promised
A puppy from the president,
And the nation waited patiently
To meet the canine resident.
Would it be a pug,
a Pomeranian, or a poodle?
A beagle, a bloodhound,
a shih tzu, or a schnoodle?
Would it be a rescue dog,
Or a pure-bred dog at that?
Or maybe he was bluffing
And they'd end up with a cat!
The public speculated
Until the dog day finally came.
Bo, their Portie water pooch,
Quickly rose to fame!

Presidential Stats

TERM: 2009–

FIRST LADY: Michelle LaVaughn Robinson Obama

VICE PRESIDENT: Joseph R. Biden, Jr.

POLITICAL PARTY: Democrat

BORN: August 4, 1961 (Honolulu, Hawaii)

OCCUPATION BEFORE PRESIDENCY: Director of the Developing Communities Project in Chicago, law professor, member of the U.S. Senate

NICKNAMES: Barry, No Drama Obama

Tell Me More!

✳ Bo Obama is a Portie, a Portuguese water dog, who was a present from Senator Ted Kennedy.

✳ Bo is hypoallergenic, which means he doesn't shed. This is important because First Daughter Malia is allergic to most dogs.

✳ Bo's favorite food is tomatoes.

✳ Obama was awarded the Nobel Peace Prize in 2009 for strengthening international diplomacy.

✳ In 2013, Bo became a big brother when the Obamas adopted Sunny, a female Portuguese water dog.

Accomplishments & Events

✳ Put a plan in place to pull American troops out of Iraq.

✳ Appointed the first Latina (Sonia Sotomayor) to the Supreme Court.

✳ Signed health care reform legislation in March 2010.

✳ Authorized the Navy SEAL raid of a compound in Pakistan in May 2011. This raid resulted in the capture and death of the terrorist Al-Qaeda leader, Osama bin Laden.

✳ Defeated Republican nominee Mitt Romney and was reelected for a second term in 2012.

INDEX